WOODEN CROSS
IRON CROSS

I promise you…

Nathalie Hervé

DEDICATION

To all those, friends, relatives or anonymous, who teach us, throughout our lives, to be better.

TABLE OF CONTENTS

INTRODUCTION

Committed, without language, with offbeat humor and sometimes incisive style,
this collection of texts is an invitation to reflection
on social facts at the heart of the news.

*"Calling women "the weaker sex" is libel; it is the injustice of the man towards the
woman.
If non-violence is the law of humanity, the future belongs to women."*

Gandhi

FOR BETTER AND FOR WORSE

For better and for worse.
This is what they promised each other in church.
He wants the best, she wants the least worst.
So be it...

He cannot live without his wife.
Without it, it is halved.
He is like a devotee without a soul.
Like an unarmed troufion.

A lease that she's finished working.
She should be home already.
JPP News is over.
Dinner is waiting for her on the table.

He is pacing up and down.
Go round and round like a lion in a cage.
Unable to reach her on her cell phone.
He puts himself in the head.

Maybe she's flirting with someone else?
To give him a little on the back.
To put a knife in the contract.
To take him for the stuffing turkey.

She, for her part, is driving her car.

It was a dry card between several vehicles.
No way to reach her husband.
No more battery on his laptop.

Everything is jostling in his head.
Will he still give her a fit of jealousy?
Throwing horrors in her face.
Fuck up twenty years of marriage.

For better and for worse.
This is what they promised each other in church.
He wants the best, she wants the least worst.
So be it...

I SAW AND I ZAPPED

I saw the TV news at supper time.
Deadly attacks, S files involved.
Recidivist rapists, overbooked prisons.
Homeless people without life, unoccupied housing.
I had trouble swallowing, I zapped...

I saw sitcoms and reality shows.
Modest scenarios, high fees.
Dolls on inflated, silicone version.
Blablabla raplapla, oversized egos.
I didn't want to see more, I zapped...

I saw the shows in the first part of the evening.
Unbearable news items, uninteresting TV films.
Farmers in need of love, Robinsonians in search of notoriety.
Talk shows where the word is loose, clashes that make people talk.
I banged my fist on the table, I zapped...

I saw the CSA rife, the rectifiers of wrong, the fear of speaking.
The rigorous teleprompter, the editing that corrects, the cut scenes.
Thought under control, freedom of expression threatened, speech censored.
The disclosures, the media exposure, the invasion of privacy.
I took a deep breath, I zapped...

I saw the reports and documentaries late at night.
The tiger mosquito, influenza A, mad cow, HIV, coronavirus.

Ivory hunting, caged animals, endangered species.
Water pollution, the industrial lobby, contaminated food.
I felt the psychosis come over me, I zapped...

I saw the dehumanization, the SMS and the mistakes in French.
Racism, war, mines, mutilated kids.
The registration number of the unemployed, the undocumented barefoot people.
Unaccompanied minors who are rejected, stateless people who are left out.
I joined my imaginary friends on the net, I zapped...

I saw the elitism of some and society outcasts.
The herdsmen, the sheep of Panurge.
The corrupt politicians, the people who pay the price.
The bosses who make profit, the purchasing power that goes downhill.
I cursed my condition as a housewife, I zapped...

AS USUAL

As usual, he comes home late from work.
Dark circles, tired face.
Strained all over, the back in compote.
And as always, it's the same old story.

He tells me he's on the verge of sending it all off.
That his job as a specialized salesperson no longer makes him dream.
That he should never have chosen the produce department.
He's got his back selling cucurbits to squash.

That he's got it on top of the lemon in his nutty schedules.
Let him work like crazy for a pittance.
That he can no longer be the turnip of service.
That his department manager is a top slacker.

That the customers take the cabbage with their stupid questions.
It's not rocket science to differentiate a curly from a batavia.
That silly jokes about cucumbers is enough.
That they all have a chickpea in the kohlrabi.

That food waste is starting to do well.
Have enough of the ugly fruits that wither in their corner.
They piss off their imported products stuffed with pesticides.
That all this petty traffic is the big deal for the big brands.

As usual, I too put my two cents in there.

Tired of my day, the treaties drawn.
Sore all over, mashed back.
And as always, it's the same old story.

I tell him that I too have seen green and unripe ones today.
That I made the elder's cereal bowl.
Bottle-fed the little one before running to school.
Messed up rags and trifles with pipelettes in a stroller.

Dust the furniture, vacuumed it.
Scoured the pans and casseroles, singing like a saucepan.
Prepared the meal with all my stock of vegetables for the winter.
Took a trip to and from the grocery store, two laundry and one coffee break.

That I have repeatedly typed stupid cartoons of the little one.
That the tutures which make vroom vroom, it starts to do well.
That my nose is full of wiping noses and asses full of shit.
I'm fed up with taking on the role of the perfect housewife.

It would be nice, from time to time, if the tasks were shared.
I'm so sick of being the only one looking after the kids.
That one of these four, by dint of abuse, I'm going to throw it all away.
He'll just have to find another ninny to serve him as a maid.

As usual, with his tail between his legs, he leaves on his own.
On the evening program, the bedroom where he will sit in front of the TV.
As usual, without taking care of him, I go for the opposite.
The night's program is the sofa in the living room where I play the film backwards.

WOODEN CROSS, IRON CROSS

More than three years of glue life.
Highs in snatches, a lot of low blows.
A planned marriage that will never happen.
Especially no children on the program.

Him, senior manager in the public service.
Senior responsibilities with a team to manage.
Workdays when stress is at its peak.
Returns to the fold where he needs his dose of alcohol.

Me, secretary in a company on a human scale.
Versatile at all levels, on all floors.
Sometimes a file to deal with, sometimes a coffee to serve.
A box in deficit, a job paid with a slingshot.

As for the lifestyle, not too much to complain about.
A luxury five-star villa in an upscale neighborhood.
A leather interior sports car for Mister.
A high-end designer kitchen for Madame.

A beginning of relationship without waves or clouds.
A climate less and less lenient over time.
More and more rare outings for two.
One-to-one evenings under pressure.

A couple's life where we avoid each other as much as possible.

A pernicious violence that takes root in everyday life.
Burst of insults that fall on my head.
Murderous attacks that touch me right in the heart.

The same arguments he puts back on the table.
A dinner that was too salty, a skirt that was too tight.
A mug in the sink, a badly ironed shirt.
A ball in the pâté, a bone in the soup.

Always the same chorus, always the same refrain.
He tells me I'm a shit, a good-for-nothing.
A slut, a bitch, a michto, a bitch.
Something without interest, something without importance.

After the incisive words, the sharp acts.
A first slap that he flanks me by surprise.
Right, left like in a ring.
Traitorous kicks that knock me down.

End of the storm in the midst of tears and chaos.
He tells me in a calm voice that it's all my fault.
That I looked for him, that he should not be provoked.
That by playing with his nerves, "well done for me!"

Life resumes its course, everything is mixed up in my head.
To admit to others the intimacy of my life, too humiliating.
File a complaint at the risk of reprisals, no thank you.
Going back to my parents' hooks, not easy.

I hate what he is, what I have become.
I hate myself for not having the strength to react.
To be just a shadow of myself.
Wanting to fuck me up.

One day, I'm ready to pack up.
The day after, I give him one last chance.
One step forward, ten steps back.
Race results, back to square one.

Over time, the blows redouble in violence.

He tells me he loves me taller than the Eiffel Tower.
Apologies like a four year old kid for hurting my head.
Swear to me "wooden cross, iron cross!", never to hurt me again.

12

THE BLONDE SMOKER

He's a cigarette addict.
He needs his package a day.
As soon as he gets up he's a little upset.
Whether he has nothing to do or has done too much, he smokes.

Cigarettes hold no secrets for him.
He knows her inside out.
This is his second wife.
Something precious that he handles with care.

She, for her part, makes him see all the colors.
She leads him by the tip of her nose.
Makes him dependent on her roundness, her curves.
Makes him her slave, her rug, her thing, her pet doggie.

It degrades it, burns it slowly.
He messes up the brain, lungs, heart, arteries.
His fingers and teeth are yellow.
Charge his breath.

He only sees through her.
It's his drug, his sweet poison.
His gigolette with less hassles.
His blonde by day, his beauty by night.

The whole time he smokes, his wife has a toast.

Smoke creeps everywhere.
It fits into every corner of the house.
Mark its territory.

Butts are piling up in ashtrays.
Every time his wife empties one, it's another that fills up.
She suffocates, she coughs.
She takes it all in the lungs.

She insists that he start weaning.
Buys him patches, gums, tablets, nicotine inhalers.
She is doing everything to put him back on the right track.
Everything to make him the perfect little husband.

She would like to model it in her image.
Make him her slave, her rug, her thing, her pet doggie.
But with her, it doesn't work.
Nothing works.

FASHION VICTIM

It was the fashion for over-inflated breasts.
So me straight up said "yes" to the mammoplasty.
Suddenly, I went to a 110 D.
Of course I turned heads!

It was the fashion for plumped lips.
So me straight up said "yes" to lipofilling.
Suddenly my mouth doubled in size.
Of course I made more than one salivate!

It was the fashion for wrinkle-free foreheads.
So me bluntly said "yes" to botox injections.
Suddenly, no more frown lines.
Of course the cougar started hunting!

It was the fashion for little noses.
So me straight up said "yes" to rhinoplasty.
Suddenly I made a plastic doll.
Of course I took selfies!

It was the fashion for drawn skins.
So me straight up said "yes" for a facelift.
Suddenly I became a show biz star.
Of course I had a lot of people at my feet!

It was the fashion for plump glutes.

So me straight up said "yes" to the prostheses.
So all of a sudden I was doing reality TV.
Of course I make the ratings!

It was the fashion for fatty blood.
So me straight up said "yes" to liposuction.
Suddenly I lost my saddlebags.
Of course I wore leggings!

It was the fashion for the big comeback.
So me straight up begged the medics to give me back my original looks.
Suddenly, no way to satisfy my whims.
Of course since then everything has to be redone in my head.

THE NARCISSISTIC PERVERT

He sees you as easy prey.
Looks out for you without missing a beat.
Analyze your weaknesses back and forth.
You stick to your ass like a morbach.

He gives you his charming number.
Put the package there even if it means making crates.
Take out his acting game like in a commedia dell'arte.
Seen taller than six feet tall.

It catches you all fire all flames in its nets.
Also deprives you of your freedom.
Grapples on you with impunity.
Pump your energy to the point of total exhaustion.

It confines you to your role as a housewife.
Convinces you of the merits of raising his offspring.
Puts you in the wheel in your quest for independence.
Positions himself as a superhero on the pretext that he supports the household.

He doesn't give you more interest than a goat poop.
Forget all the opportunities to please yourself.
Showeres you with compliments without saving his saliva.
Play the perfect husbands fair in public.

It isolates you from others like a bird makes its nest.

Convinces you of the harmfulness of those around you.
Highlights what is wrong with you.
Works to get you under his control quickly.

It adapts to each situation depending on the person.
Invent himself a life to be up to his interlocutor.
Take out his megalomaniac side to wow the gallery.
Shows off at his best to gain favor.

He seduces with his beautiful words and his charming number.
Can use humor when the rewards are worth the effort.
Makes you promises in the wind just to save time.
Arrange to tell you what you want to hear.

He knows how to be persuasive to get what he wants.
Do not hesitate to play the victim to soften you.
Works you on the body until you give in.
Be aggressive if you resist him.

He only thinks of flattering his ego.
He invented bac plus ten diplomas and prestigious titles.
Don't skimp on spending while it's on him.
Pavane in the most chic clothes.

He expresses himself confusedly when going from rooster to donkey.
Has trouble understanding his lies.
Play bad faith even if it means making yourself look like a fool.
Sends you on the roses to make you rise in tension.

He hates anyone who gets in his way.
Can't stand the thought that we can leave him.
Bludgeon you with threats to destroy you.
Make your life hell if you resist him.

He or she, regardless of gender.
Whatever the different facets of his character.
A single name under this complex personality.
The narcissistic pervert manipulator.

THE CASHIER

I am a cashier.
Not anywhere my little lady.
In the most popular hyper in the region.
For one of the biggest brands.

Uniform required.
Smooth hair at the top.
Red on the nails.
As much on the lips.

Smile in reading mode.
Kids on stand-by.
Hot in front of my little chickens!
The great Zaza makes its entrance.

Nine sharp hours.
The sales have started.
Security is on the alert.
The iron curtain is up.

There is excitement in the store.
Customers are pouring in from all sides.
The assault on the shelves is on.
Steel wagons wage war on each other.

Find the right deal at all costs.

Even if it means tearing the articles out of their hands.
It goes: "I saw it first! "
And tralali and tralalère, na!

Once you've finished shopping, head to the checkouts.
There, endless queues.
It doubles as kindergarten kids.
And nanani and nananère, na!

The articles parade on the carpet.
Customers follow each other in single file.
Never the same heads.
Always the same old story.

Sometimes, first-price items.
Sometimes, premium products.
Sometimes, it counts the pennies.
Sometimes, it snaps at ease.

I am a cashier.
I am paid to cash.
Each his shit, God for all.
And tralali and tralalère, na!

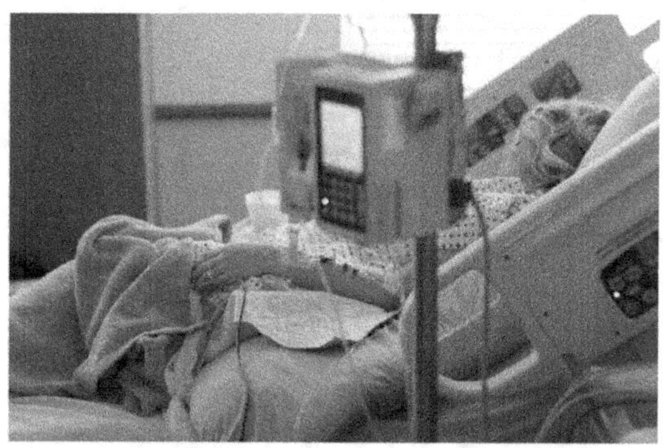

CHARCOT DISEASE

A family meal that is most banal.
On the menu of the day, something digestible.
As a main course, the next summer vacation.
For dessert, my box of camembert which gets carried away.

Impossible to articulate anything.
Words refuse to be heard.
No more control over my mouth.
It's autopilot in my head.

Maybe a stroke.
A whole series of exams to find out.
An electromyogram, an MRI.
Blood and urine tests, a lumbar puncture.

A definitive diagnosis of amyotrophic lateral sclerosis.
Charcot's disease in other words.
Not the spinal form but the bulbar form.
An incurable neurodegenerative disease.

The muscles of the mouth are the first to be affected.
The first signs of weakness in the legs are there.
No other alternatives than progressive paralysis.
A life expectancy limited to more or less three years.

Several treatments on the program.

Riluzole to scratch a few months of life.
Illusory consultations with the speech therapist.
Hopeful sessions with my magnetizer.

A stone's throw from retirement, it's total regression.
I wear a baby bib so much I salivate.
I don't give a damn all over me drinking through a straw.
I speak on a slate like in a small school.

The risk of taking a wrong turn is fearful for my life.
My weight loss no longer gives me a choice.
I go to the pool table for a gastrostomy.
For the tracheostomy, no need to put it back on the table.

The disease is eating away at it, consuming all my energy.
I have less and less strength in my arms.
My legs are finding it harder and harder to support me.
I move with a walker.

On the mental side, it's a mess in my head.
I alternate periods of depression and fits of giggles.
My three-year reprieve is coming to an end.
My magnetizer is no miracle worker.

I am on non-invasive ventilation day and night.
I'm at the height of what I can take.
My husband accompanies me to the emergency department.
The whole family arrives at my bedside.

A rattle echoed in the cold and narrow room.
The priest wears Extreme Unction while reciting "our father".
The hospital room is gradually regaining its calm.
The successive doses of morphine gradually take effect.

THE EVE OF CHRISTMAS

It's Christmas Eve.
The gifts are under the tree.
Those of Uncle Henry who amaze the gallery.
The others who do not make noise in their corner.

Everyone is on their thirty-one.
We brought out the sequins and the evening wear.
The family photos, the most beautiful smiles.
Memories of when everything was fine.

All the usual stuff is on the table.
The oyster platter, the smoked salmon.
Toast with foie gras, champagne flutes.
Golden paper napkins.

As an aperitif, a royal kir.
As a main course, a capon stuffed with foie gras.
As an accompaniment, roasted potatoes Swedish style.
For dessert, a chocolate log with buttercream.

All the guests are gathered around the table.
Grandfather reigns as a patriarch.
Grandmother is conspicuous by her absence.
The kids dig into the box of chocolates.

Ah! In-laws!

Always the same heads.
Always the same specimens.
Small round table story to set the scene.

In front of me, my cousin Geraldine, all out of place.
False nose, false nails, false mouth, false breasts.
Real plague.
More urban than her, you die.

Executive secretary, Madame has everything in the right order.
A successful marriage, a beautiful hut.
A nice guy, good chic good kind, good in all respects.
Two super clean cherubs promoted to great careers.

To my left, straight on landed from his Normandy.
At the wheel of its large displacement all options.
On the arm of her one hundred percent superficial pin-up.
Uncle Henry, the fat beauf first class.

He's the old facho idiot.
Self-employed butcher-butcher-caterer.
Just divorced, quickly recovered.
In search of relationships, "no fuss".

To my right, Tony, my brother.
At his side, the one who shares his life.
Open-minded with great ease of speaking.
Modest when it comes to talking about himself.

At the end of the table, my cousin Fabrice.
Straight out of his military barracks.
On perm for several weeks.
In an already well advanced state of alcoholism.

Everywhere else, kids and their cellphones.
Busy looking at things that make them laugh.
To take selfies while taking the break.
Add filters to show off a max.

It is my cousin Geraldine who launches hostilities.

She asks me youngster if I have a "crush".
Add that it is time to put the ring on my finger.
Joke by insisting that I am on course to end up an old maid.

Uncle Henry leans into the discussion.
He points out that sometimes celibacy is okay.
That my last flirt was not terrible.
That in addition to having a tanned complexion, he sulked at pork in block.

Tony, like a big brother, comes to my rescue.
He says that true love has no color.
That Uncle Bernard pisses us off with his pig.
He better stick his nose in the slaughterhouses a little more.

Grandfather ends the discussion.
The Christmas log lifts the atmosphere.
The fireplace warms the room.
Fabrice drops off in his corner.

Only a few hours before midnight mass in freezing cold.
Soon the liver attacks over the toilet bowl.
Tomorrow morning, the "not even pretty" presents and the hangover.
Long live the magic of Christmas!

SNAGS ON THE SCREEN

My father is the king of loose watching TV.
Reports, series, talk shows, news channels, it's all there.
He gorges himself on images until he can no longer sleep at night.
He watches in replay everything he couldn't see.

My mother is a beauty YouTuber.
Thousands of people subscribed to his channel.
Always more fans on social networks.
24 hours, it is online.

Me, I make my life on my side.
I don't weigh heavily in their daily life.
I am half of thirty years old.
I barely exist.

My own refuge is my room.
I have everything a kid could want.
A TV, a state-of-the-art game console.
A tablet, an iPhone, a laptop.

What I love most is my game console.
Above all, a game that has just been released.
Basically, you have to save the world by killing a lot of zombies.
Frankly, it's too great!

I play it all my free time with my friends.

Once in the game, it's not easy to get out.
When I win, it's the "floss dance" in my head.
When I lose, I drummer because I have so much rage.

From there, my parents arrive in fury.
My dad tells me to mute it.
My mother threatens to deny me any outings.
Everyone leaves to go about their own business.

I am a pure product of the 2000s.
A gnian-gnian generation is addicted to online games.
A fifteen-year-old kid disconnected from his parents.
I am alone on earth.

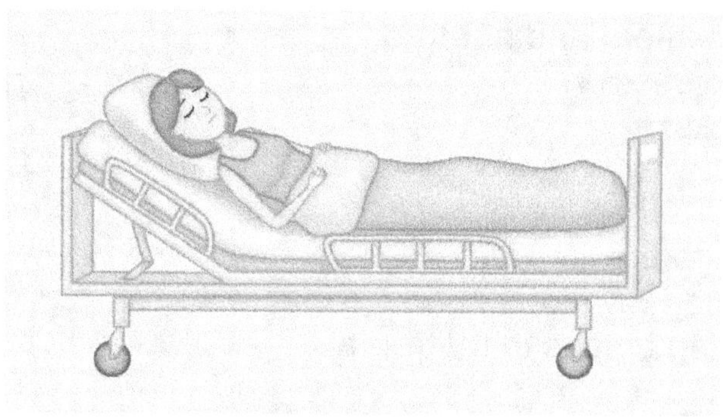

TICK-TOCK

High-risk pregnancy service.
Two weeks of hospitalization.
My water bag is cracked.
Oligoamnios is confirmed.
Formal prohibition to get up.

Tick-Tock.
Seven sharp hours.
Bright light in my face.
The direct-to-ear thermometer.
On the temperature side, everything is ok.

Knock. Knock.
The breakfast service arrives.
Rusk coffee for Madame.
Orange juice in bricks.
A little prunes for the transit.

Knock. Knock.
A student nurse already well established.
With it, an electronic blood pressure monitor on wheels.
Quick start of the device.
In terms of figures, R.A.S.

Knock. Knock.
It's time for a personal toilet.

In front of my frifri an intern and her tutor.
Educational cleaning session.
I squeeze the buttocks.

Knock. Knock.
A new head for monitoring.
Two sensors placed on my stomach.
The sound of galloping horses in the room.
I loosen my teeth.

Knock. Knock.
General tour for debriefing.
At the head of the line the doctor.
In his hands, a whole bunch of papelards.
Behind him, all his flock of students.

Knock. Knock.
Check-up with the gynecologist on duty.
Generous layer of gel on my lower abdomen.
Artistic slides with an ultrasound probe.
Zoom in close up just to be sure.

Tick. Tock.
The time has come for the verdict.
The diagnosis of anamnios is confirmed.
Medical termination of pregnancy is required.
There is nothing more to do.

THE WISE MONKEYS

I heard my neighbor cry for help under the blows of her husband.
I was told, "Shhh, shut it up! Mind what concerns you!"
I pretended I hadn't heard anything, I didn't say anything.
Since then, I can't sleep.

I heard the kid next door getting beaten up by his stepfather.
I was told, "Shhh, shut it up! You may be on the wrong track!"
I pretended I hadn't heard anything, I didn't say anything.
Since then, I don't know where I am.

I saw the old woman in front of my flat covered in bruises.
I was told, "Shhh, shut it up! I Don't be fooled by appearances!"
I acted as if I had seen nothing, I said nothing.
I have since lost my appetite.

I saw a poor guy get stabbed under my windows.
I was told, "Shhh, shut it up! You might get into trouble!"
I acted as if I had seen nothing, I said nothing.
Since then, I have struggled to live.

In the midst of my depression, I wanted to end it.
Emergency consultation with a shrink.
Quick assessment from the first session.
There is only one remedy to heal: open my mouth.

Immediate practice with my next door neighbor.

A quick phone call to Violences Femmes Info 3919.
Shortly after, my neighbor packed up.
Since then, I have no more insomnia.

I followed up with the kid next door.
A quick and well-made call to 119 Allo Enfance en Danger.
Shortly after, social services arrived.
Since then, things have been better in my head.

I continued with the old woman in front of my flat.
An anonymous phone call to 3977, Allo Maltraitance des Gens Agées.
Soon after, no more housekeepers around.
I have since regained my appetite.

I'm done with the poor guy killed in the street.
A quick trip to the police station to find out the identity of the attacker.
Shortly after, an indictment for intentional homicide.
Since then, I have regained a taste for life.

STORY WITHOUT WORDS

He is as dumb as a carp.
Impossible to tear the worms out of his nose.
As closed as an endangered scallop.
He stubbornly refuses to open up.

She is paddling with him.
She goes straight adrift.
Sometimes she takes him for a fool who has nothing to say.
Sometimes for an impostor who has something to hide.

The more he is deaf, the more she screams in his ears.
Everything is controversial.
Her dirty panties on the floor, her allergy to dishes.
His burps lightly, his farts with impunity.

Him, on his side cash.
Like the defendant in his cubicle, he has nothing to add.
What do you want him to tell her?
Doesn't doubt benefit the accused?

That he's fed up with this big one.
That he can no longer see her in painting.
That he cheated on her as soon as her back is turned.
That he stay with her for the comfort of the house and the drinking food.

No, he chose to remain silent as a carp.

No buoy for her, no lifeboat, no distress rocket.
The winds are with him, she can still row.
And come what may!

NA NA NI, NA NA NA

Yeh! I'm on a dating site.
Sniff! A lease that I am divorced.
Hush! A bit of patter for my profile.
Uh! Some slightly faked photos.
Oops! Not easy to bait men my age.

Yep! First physical selection.
Mmm! I scroll through the paper clips.
Ouaaa! I flash on him, I click.
Yes! We like each other, it matches.
Yum! I will see his profile in more detail.

Tralala! First written exchanges.
Yuck! Too many mistakes get stuck.
Blah blah blah! Too much chat, that tiresome.
Hmmm! Lack of tact, I pass.
Ouch! Thirst for sex, I skip.

Yahou! First face to face on the webcam.
Tada! Total surprise of his physique.
Ugh! Deception on the merchandise.
Pfff! Unpacking a little too shameless.
Eho! I don't eat that bread!

Hop! First meeting in a bar.
Phew! Too well undermined, I love it.

Fart! Confidence, I let go.
Ha ha! Good dose of humor, I smile.
Ron Ron! Tactile reconciliation, I let myself be.

Hin han! First meeting at the hotel.
Tchin! Toast with champagne.
Smack! Our mouths are racing.
Oust! Impasse on the preliminaries.
Bof! Quite a bit of progress to be made.

Flop! Review of this story.
Ark! No news from the playboy.
Huh! Still active on the site.
Baff! That's all he deserves.
Gnagnagna! I got screwed.

I LOVE HIM SO MUCH

I love him so much that he's mine.
No way he'll slip through my fingers.
On the lookout for his every move.
By dint of coping, we get into trouble.

A text he receives in the middle of the night.
Whoever it is, I must elude the mystery.
Evasive explanations, I go hunting.
By dint of searching, we find anything.

Him in the bathroom, I stick my nose in his tablet.
Incognito, direct the history of his research.
There, "sick jealousy" comes up several times.
By dint of nosing around, you come across what you don't want.

The geolocation of his cell phone is activated.
I start zooming in all the places he goes.
I learn that he is secretly preparing a surprise for me.
By dint of imagining the worst, we sometimes drink a cup.

I find myself rummaging in the pockets of his clothes.
To check the details of his bank statements.
To check in detail all his dressing room.
By dint of playing the detectives, we invent ourselves a culprit.

The smell of perfume, a blond hair on his jacket.

His silences, his looks, his way of touching me.
Whatever he does, whatever he says, everything about him is suspect.
By dint of looking for the little beast, we end up waking the animal.

The reproaches and insults that we swing in the face.
The punches in the wall that slaughter his fingers.
The marital bed he leaves for the company of his friends.
By dint of taking it in, he ends up running away from the shit.

The more he avoids me, the more my fits of jealousy intensify.
Decision made, he no longer wants to make his life with me.
Completely devastated, I understand that there is nothing more to do.
By dint of playing with his nerves, he ended up packing his bags.

COLLATERAL DAMAGE

Years in the same box.
End of my maternity leave.
The time for recovery has come.
It's not easy to get back on track.

A welcome not the friendliest.
We avoid meeting my gaze.
Not the slightest interest in me.
Everyone remains focused on their work.

I am not at the end of my surprises.
A new head occupies my office.
All my personal belongings are gone.
No way to find out more.

Neither one nor two, I will see the boss directly.
He's texting me that no one is irreplaceable.
That in business, as in the private sector, sometimes you have to make choices.
That before getting pregnant you had to think twice.

Here I am returned to a room that serves as a storage room.
A few square meters of surface, a table, a chair.
No one to talk to, no windows to the outside.
In the middle of the archive boxes, I am put in the closet.

Without work tools, it's difficult to spend your days.

The only distraction is a ticking clock.
For unique visits, the boss's exhausting thoughts.
The only ambition is to wait for time to pass.

Submit my resignation, it is out of the question.
I end up having a depression that takes me straight to the doctor.
Rebelote for a work stoppage of several weeks.
On my return, the tensions with the chef increased.

In addition to moral harassment, there is physical violence.
I contact the prud'hommes who need testimonials.
There, my co-workers are all unanimous.
Impossible to alienate the management because of the consequences.

Alone against all, I fight with the means at hand.
Camera hidden in the room, recorder stashed in my bag.
With the evidence in my pocket, I move on to the final step.
Chat with the boss in a memorable one-on-one.

He is all smiles as he hands me a breach of contract.
It is all smiles that I tell him that I have seized the prud'hommes.
That I have in my possession enough to blow him and his box.
That before charging me for my pregnancy, you had to think twice.

FUNNY LIFE

I'm Jojo the pretty little goldfish.
In my makeshift jar, I blow bubbles.
Nothing else to do but go around in circles.
While the kids knock on the glass.

I'm Titi the singing goldfinch.
Deprived of my freedom, I look good behind bars.
Nothing else to do but whistle on my perch.
While my kidnapper trades me for a high price.

I'm Mimi the tiny hamster.
In my plastoc cage, it's frankly misery.
Nothing else to do than play acrobats.
While the kids admire my exploits.

I am Soso the corn snake.
In my terrarium, no more rodents to hunt.
Nothing else to do but wait for the peck.
While the kids contemplate the show.

I am Nunuche the boniche at home.
In my high tower, it's really a struggle.
Nothing else to do but do chores.
While my Jules watches me at work.

ALL IS SAID

One in 100 risk of miscarriage after amniocentesis.
Trust me! Everything will be fine.
This is what this gynecologist told me between two consultations.
Head down, I let myself be carried away by his experience.
The intervention screwed up, no other option but the IMG.
All is said!

You have been granted 100 percent legal aid.
Trust me! I will give you my legal support.
This is what this lawyer told me between two interviews.
Head down, I accepted his help in asserting my rights.
Sloppy file, nothing was done to defend my interests.
All is said!

Great idea for choosing our world famous brand.
Trust me dearest! I will take your career off the ground.
That's what this senior CEO told me between two business meetings.
Head down, I shared a drink with him, letting my guard down.
On the strength of my fragility, the BCBG raped me with impunity.
All is said!

Here we do not joke with school bullying.
Trust me! Your child is in good hands.
This is what this CPE threw at me between two coffee breaks.
Head down, I turned it over to this woman on the ground.
From bad to worse, my daughter ended up making a suicide attempt.

All is said!

You did well to file a complaint for domestic violence.
Trust me! We will do everything to protect you.
That's what that agent threw at me between piles of files.
Head down, I had total faith in this strong man.
Short-lived respite, the fatal blow struck me in stride.
All is said!

You are the dearest thing to me in the world.
Trust me darling! You and me it's forever.
This is what this fagot told me between two sessions of inflating.
Head down, I said "YES!" to the regime of the universal community.
All that to divorce in the wake by giving him a good part of my fortune.
All is said!

Come and make papouilles and guili-guili to your darling daddy!
Trust me my princess! You know I love you.
That's what my father threw at me between two glasses of whiskey.
Head down, I took his grown-up word.
Years of being raped under the watchful eye of my mother.
All is said!

A JOB AT ALL COSTS

I have been looking for a job for months.
The refusals, I wipe them out, one after the other.
At forty brooms, it's not easy to get hired.
Like a messed up fruit, I am quarantined.

Job interview for a secretary position.
With enthusiasm, I unpack everything on the table.
My baccalaureate, my patter, my Ultra White smile.
My generous cleavage, my good humor, my jobs here and there.

Against all odds, the job is for me.
This is an SME in the IT field.
A full-time job paid with a slingshot.
An administrative task to assist the management.

Neither one nor two, the boss plunges me straight into the bath.
A pile of files to process, a ton of tidying up.
The standard to manage, its full-bodied coffee, its character to bear.
His schedule to organize, his letters to rank in order of importance.

Not the slightest moment of respite, not the slightest misstep.
Glued non-stop to my basques, the boss makes me misery.
Everything I do must be in keeping with his expectations.
Everything I say must be clearly rephrased in correct French.

As a master of perfection, he forgives me nothing.

Archive files should be arranged in chronological order.
Its customer meetings must be perfectly legible.
My delays of a few minutes must be seriously justified.

The more I lose in efficiency, the more it overloads me with work.
The more productivity he loses, the more I work overtime.
Under pressure, I make mistakes worth me a warning.
Exhausted, I end up having the nerves that let go.

Dead beat, I start whining about anything.
At the lowest of my ability, I can't do much anymore.
Overwhelmed by the situation, it is with a knot that I go to work.
Exhausted at the end of my day, it's on my knees that I go home.

Once at home, it is with sleeping pills that I fall asleep.
Until this day, when I ended up in the ER for an overdose of pills.
Saved by a phone call, I learn from the doctor that I am having a burnout.
As for that decisive phone call that saved my life, guess who I owe it to?

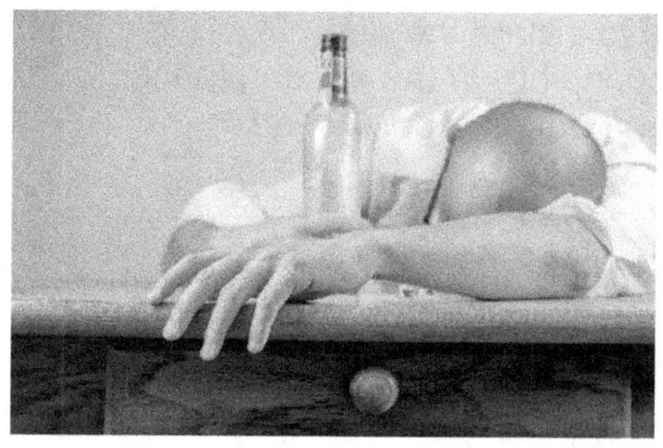

SO ADDICT

Addicted to my cell phone, I am online non-stop.
Barely standing up when I am glued to the screen.
Friends, followers, snap… on any occasion, we share.
Don't give a shit about forgetting my parents!

Addicted to alcohol, I drink at the slightest pretext.
Anywhere, need my dose of ethanol.
Whiskey, beer, vodka… alcohol in all its forms.
Don't give a damn about causing the accident!

Addict of online games, I touch my ball.
Objective number one, to be on top of the rankings.
In search of adrenaline, I rush straight for the enemy.
Don't give a fuck if my teachers are on edge!

Addicted to cigarettes, I smoke at the slightest chance.
A crooked fart, I blow in the wind.
Blondes, brunettes, rolls ... whatever.
Don't give a fuck about intoxicating my kids!

Addict of the small screen, I skip the channels.
Quiet in my sofa, I watch and I relax.
Immediate boarding, I travel outside the borders.
Don't give a shit about being the last of the lazy!

Addicted to fishing, I slip away day and night.

In river or at sea, I have to titillate the fish.
Fly, bottom, lures,… depending on the circumstances.
Don't give a fuck if my wife takes a back seat!

Addicted to drugs, I use non-stop.
A joint to start, cocaine to finish.
A risky addiction, dope at all costs.
Don't give a fuck about selling my charms for cash!

Sex addict, I can't stand still.
Expert in dredging, I shoot at all costs.
Blondes, brunettes, redheads ... it's all good to take.
Don't give a damn about a marriage that only lasts for a while!

THE LADYBUG

I'm the red ladybug with black dots.
The godly beast born under a lucky star.
I sow joy wherever I go.
I am the admiration of young and old.

I invite myself to a brooding guy.
There, a fly flutters in the air.
No time to admire him more.
And wham! A swatter in his pear.

I land on the sticky kitchen floor.
There, a cockroach crumbles as it crosses the room.
No time to encourage him more than that.
And wham! A blow of pschitt in his pipe.

I sneak inside a closet.
There, a moth hides in the middle of the food.
No time to warn her.
And wham! A rag in his face.

I isolate myself in a corner of the room.
There, a spider weaves its web.
No time to contemplate his work.
And wham! A book shot in his face.

I am the red ladybug with black dots.

The godly beast born under a lucky star.
I arouse admiration everywhere I go.
I parade like a miss to curry favor.

The guy smiles at me as he watches me pretend.
He begins to sing: "Ladybug, fly away!"
Insist, go crazy to see that I resist him.
And wham! A punch in my face.

ABOUT THE AUTHOR

Originally from the Parisian suburbs, I found refuge in the south of France where I work as a receptionist in an emergency accommodation center.

As part of my activity, I work with women victims of domestic violence, homeless people and unaccompanied foreign minors on a daily basis.

It is from these different encounters and personal experiences that I draw my inspiration.

www.ingramcontent.com/pod-product-compliance
Lightning Source LLC
Chambersburg PA
CBHW080851160726
47999CB00009B/3073